What are Thinkologie Books?

We believe in teaching language via stories. Stories bring cultural context and display regional differences as well.

Each story will be in English as well as the target foreign language. Each storybook will have an interactive book to test comprehension. The books will be in Kindle and Paperback.

This activity book is a workbook

created to go with the Kindle

version of the story.

Some 'bold' words are translated

into Hindi.

Write the answers in Hindi.

Find additional bilingual books on

our author page

https://www.amazon.com/author/

thinkologiebooks

Brainstorming Activity

Guess what the story is about by looking at the title and pictures.

Write or draw out a brief answer.

My **five-year-old daughter** पांच साल की बेटी, Mini, talks all the time. Her chatter made her mom angry, but I hated to see Mini quiet.

Early in the **morning** सुबह one day, Mini asked, "Dad, Ramdayal, the **security guard** चौकीदार calls a crow a 'krow.' He does not know anything, does he?"

Before I could explain the **answer** उत्तर to her, she

had already started to talk about **something else**

कुछ और.

"What do you **think** सोच Dad? Bhola says there is

an **elephant** हाथी in the clouds blowing **water** पानी

out of his trunk. Therefore, it **rains**, बारिश" she

said.

Again फिर, before I could answer, Mini asked me,

"Dad, what **relation** रिश्तेदार is **mother** माँ to you?"

"She is my dear, little **sister-In-law** भाभी !" I

answered, finally getting out a reply.

Joking, but with a serious **face** चेहरा, I said to her,

"Go and play with Bhola, Mini! I am busy!"

My desk was **near a window** खिड़की that looked out over the road. One day, Mini was playing near my **desk** मेज while I was writing out the **seventeenth** सत्रहवाँ chapter of my book. **Suddenly** अचानक, Mini ran to the window and shouted, "Hey, Kabuliwalla! Hey, Kabuliwalla!"

I looked out of the window and saw the Kabuliwalla. He was **walking** चल रहा था along the street, carrying his bag of **fruit** फल. He wore the **tunic and pants** कमीज और पतलून that Afghans wear along with a **turban** पगड़ी. Hearing Mini shouting, the **Kabuliwalla** काबुलीवाला looked up towards the little girl. Mini ran to her mom and hid behind her.

Mini was convinced that the Kabuliwalla carried

little kids in his big bag instead of fruits and nuts

फल और मेवे.

The Kabuliwalla came to my **door** दरवाजा and

greeted me with a smiling **face** चेहरा. I bought

some fruit and nuts from him, and we spoke

about different **things** चीज़ें.

The Kabuliwalla came bearing **stories** कहानियाँ

from afar! He spoke of the people that he had

met in his travels from **different places** अलग-

अलग स्थान.

I thought about him while I sat at my desk in my

corner कोने of Kolkata.

I imagined many **merchants** व्यापारी who

travelled on **camels and donkeys** ऊंट और गधे

over the mountains with goods while they left

their **families** परिवार at home.

I envied them in a way because they got to experience different cultures विभिन्न संस्कृतियां.

I wanted Mini to be **brave** बहादुर, so I asked her to come out and meet the Kabuliwalla. She stood next to my **chair** कुर्सी with her **eyes** आंखें fixed on him and his bag. He offered her some fruit and nuts, but Mini refused them and crept closer to me.

Mini's mom, on the **other hand** दूसरी ओर, was cautious. She did not trust the Kabuliwalla and used to beg me to be careful around him. She was **timid** डरपोक and always thought the worst about situations and people.

Before he left, Kabuliwalla would always ask about Mini. "Where is the **little girl** छोटी लड़की, Sir?" he would inquire.

Some days passed. One **morning** सुबह when I was leaving the house, I was startled to see Mini sitting near the door talking and laughing with the Kabuliwalla. She held a **handful** मुट्ठी भर of **raisins** किशमिश and **almonds** बादाम that he had given her. I gave him some money for the gift, which he accepted and slipped into his **pocket** जेब. Later, I learned that he had given the money back to Mini!

Mini and the Kabuliwalla became great **friends** मित्र. She would often joke with him. Their **conversations** बातचीत went like this:

"Kabuliwalla, what do you have in your bag?" she asked.

"An **elephant** हाथी," he answered.

"When are you going to your Father-in-law's house?" she asked him time after time.

In mock anger he would reply, "I am never going to my **father-in-law ससुर** ! I would thrash him!"

Mini would giggle and laugh at this wisecrack. It was fascinating for me to watch someone else who had the patience to chat with Mini--besides myself, of course.

The year passed by and it was winter. In January,

the Kabuliwalla usually returned to Afghanistan

to be with his family. Before he left for his home,

he would visit his **customers ग्राहक** to collect the

money they owed to him.

One morning while I was at my desk working, I heard a noise शोर from the street. It was around eight o'clock आठ बजे and there were many people outside. I looked out of the window and saw the police leading the Kabuliwalla away. Kabuliwalla looked awful; he had bloodstains खून on his clothes.

I later learned that when Kabuliwalla had tried to collect money for a shawl, the customer denied ever buying it. A **fight** लड़ाई broke out between the two men. It ended when Kabuliwalla stabbed the **man** आदमी.

Many years passed and we never heard any more about the Kabuliwalla. Mini grew up to be a **beautiful woman** सुंदर महिला and soon it was her **wedding day** विवाह का दिन. On the morning of her wedding, there was a knock on our door. To my surprise, there was the Kabuliwalla standing on our doorstep!

I was **upset** परेशान that he had shown up on such an **auspicious day** शुभ दिन especially because he had committed a **murder** हत्या. I asked him to leave.

As he turned to leave, he gave me some **fruit फल** for Mini. Then, he showed me **a tattered piece of paper कागज का फटा हुआ टुकड़ा** on which was his daughter's **handprint हस्तछाप**. I immediately felt compassion for this man. I thought about how he must have missed his own daughter's childhood.

So, I invited him to come inside and meet with Mini. My wife and I called Mini downstairs to meet with the Kabuliwalla. He was astonished to see Mini tall and grown up. He was also saddened because he remembered **his own daughter** अपनी बेटी, also Mini's age. He then told us that he loved talking to Mini because she reminded him of his own daughter back **home** घर in Afghanistan.

At that point, my wife and I decided to give him

money to return to Afghanistan and see his

daughter.

We decided to use the **money** पैसे that we would

have spent on **wedding** शादी lights for this

instead.

Write the Hindi
words for 5 year old

____

Q. What is the word for
Dad?

____

What is the word for
daughter?

____

What is the word for
Elephant?

____

What is the word for
rain?

____

What is the word for
chair?

____

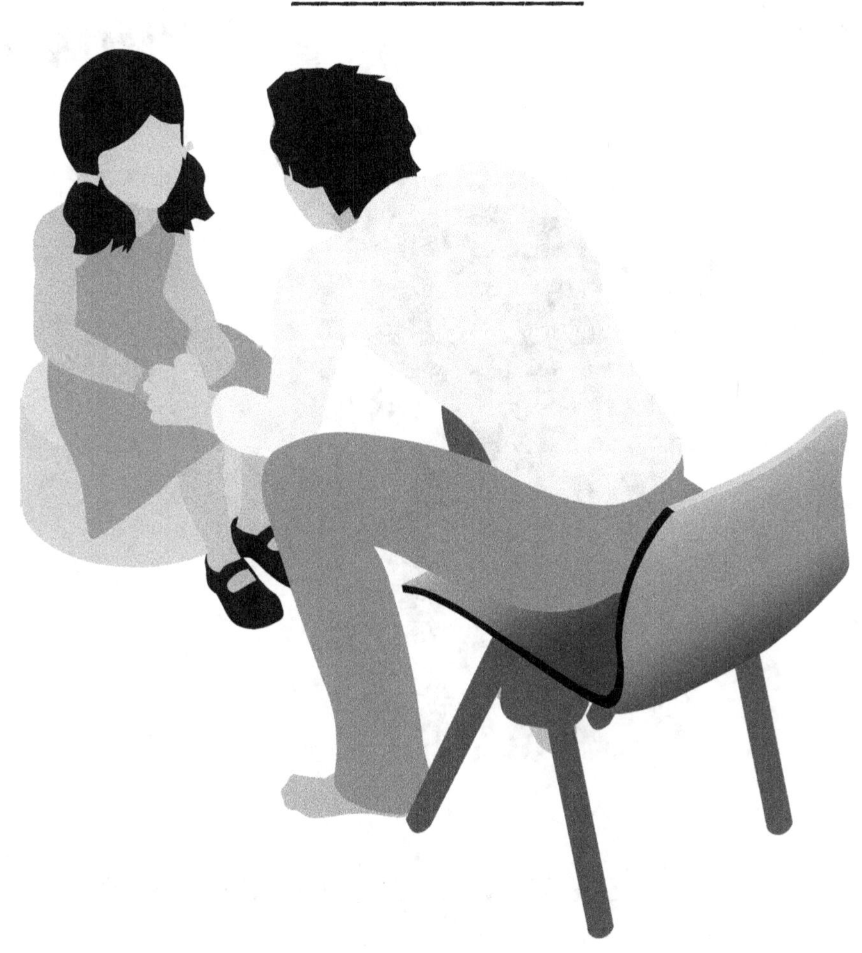

What is the word for window?

____

What is the word for

tunic?

____

What is the word for

pants?

____

What is the word for
fruit?

____

What is the word for
nuts?

____

What is the word for door?

____

What is the word for
mother?

____

How did the Kabuliwalla feel?

____

Write two words to describe Mini.

______________ and ______________

This is a picture of a _______________

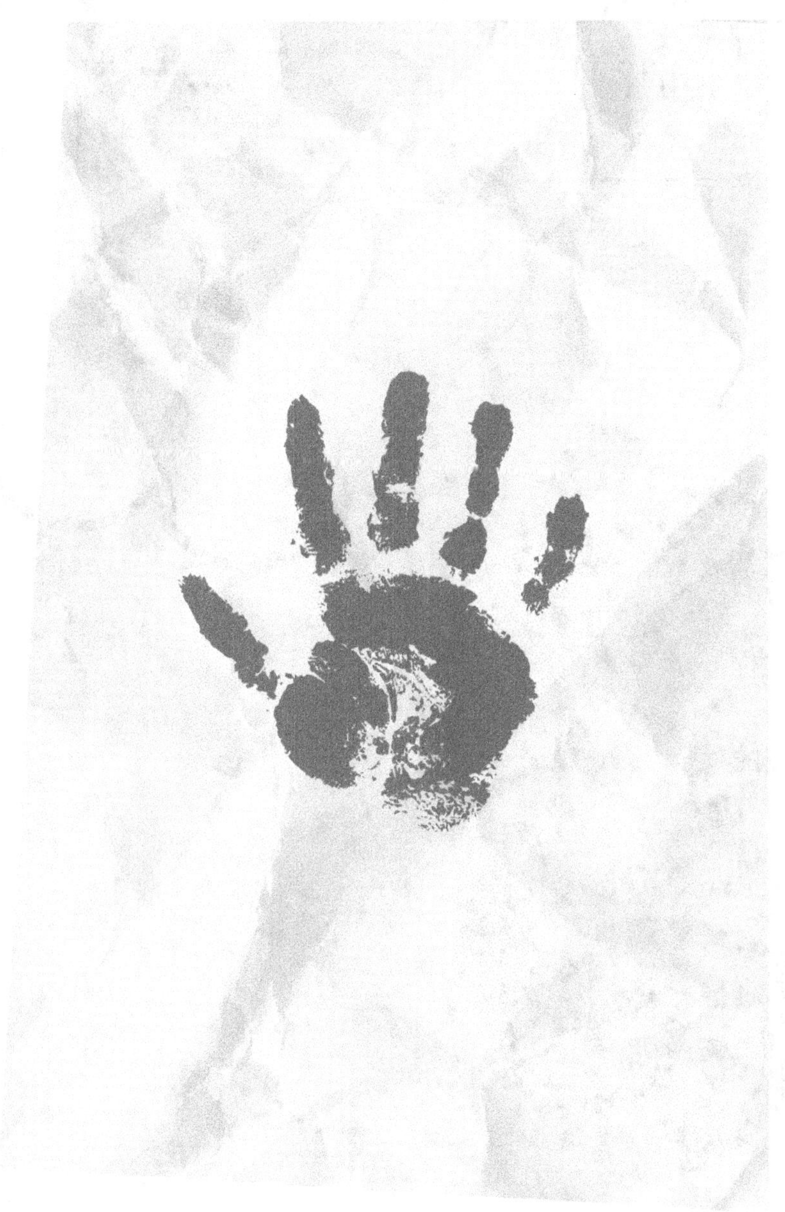

What is the word for
girl?

____

Who are these
people?

____

Who is this man?

____

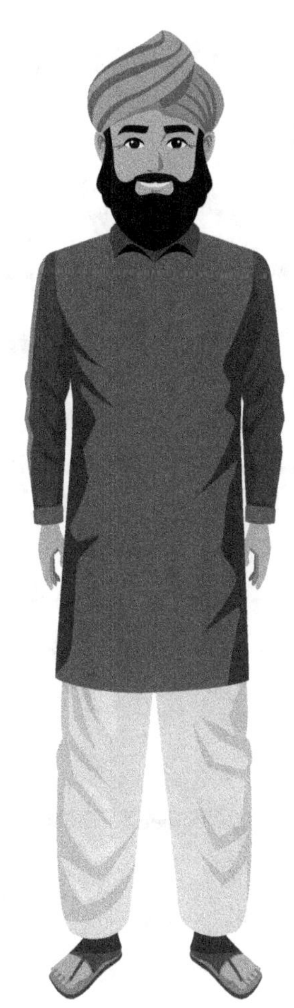

Sorting Activity

Read the text. Find and place the words in the box

Nouns	Proper Nouns
Abstract Nouns	**Collective Nouns**
Definite article	**Indefinite article**

Sorting Activity

Read the text. Find and place the words in the box

Adverbs	Verbs
Adjectives	**Prepositions**
Punctuation	**Superlatives**

Mark the Text

Use the following strategies to mark the text.

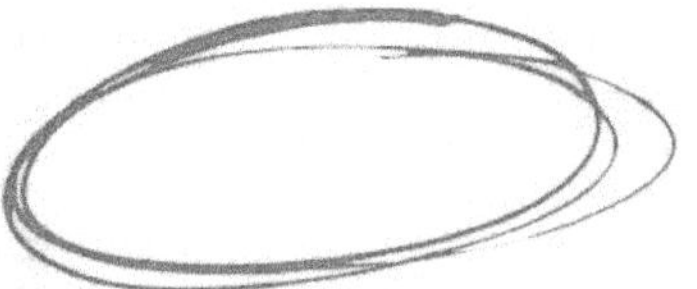

Circle content and look up the words in dictionary.com

Put a question mark near words that need explanation.

When did this story take place?

Where did this story take place?

What is the theme of this story?
e.g. love, slavery, war

Create a One Pager

Draw and Label the Story

Contact us

Our mission is to help other educators, coaches and homeschoolers also!
Contact us for customized interactive books. If you want to publish your book - contact us for that too!
Follow our author page
https://amazon.com/author/thinkologiebooks
We are also on Instagram @thinkologie
Twitter @ thinkologie
Facebook @thinkologiemedia

Thinkologie